France: 72 Fascinating Facts For Kids

Leanne Walters

This book is just one of a series of "Fascinating Facts For Kids" books. For more fascinating facts about people, history, animals and more please visit:

www.fascinatingfactsforkids.com

Contents

Where is France?

1. France is the largest country in western Europe with an area of more than 250,000 square miles (650,000 sq km). It is home to a population of more than 65 million people.

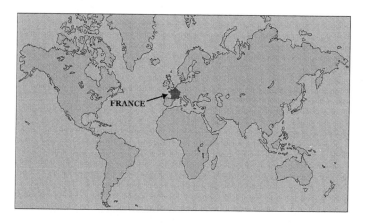

2. France shares its border with Spain, Andorra and Monaco to the south, Italy and Switzerland to the east, and Germany, Luxembourg and Belgium to the north east. Britain, which lies across the English Channel, is connected to France by the Channel Tunnel.

3. The French coastline is more than 2,100 miles (3,400 km) long and borders the Mediterranean Sea in the south, the Atlantic Ocean in the west and the English Channel in the north west.

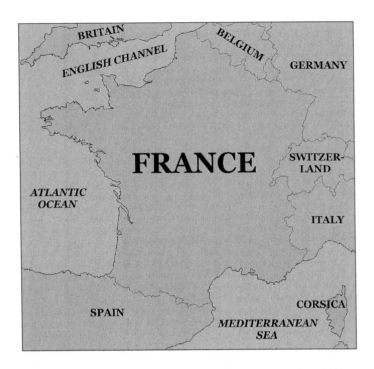

4. The Mediterranean island of Corsica, which lies 100 miles (160 km) to the south east of the mainland, is a part of France.

History

5. People have been living in what is now called France for more than 30,000 years. The first cave dwellers decorated the walls of their homes with beautiful paintings which can still be seen today.

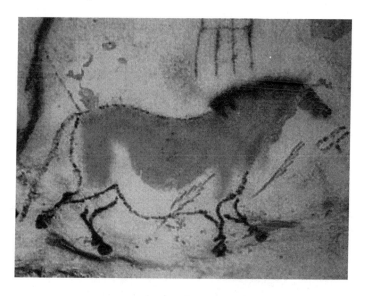

A cave painting at Lascaux

6. In the 5th century BC, France was invaded by Celtic tribes from central Europe. The Celts were great warriors and were soon fighting their new neighbors of the Roman Empire.

7. The Celts and Romans were constantly at war with each other, until, in the 1st century BC, Emperor Julius Caesar and his army conquered the country the Romans called Gaul and made it a part of the Roman Empire.

8. The Romans ruled Gaul for 500 years until they were defeated by a powerful tribe called the Franks. France gets its name from the Franks.

9. The Franks created a vast empire covering much of western Europe, which reached its pinnacle under the reign of Emperor Charlemagne in the 8th century. Following the death of Charlemagne in 814, the empire was divided into what are now France and Germany.

The Charlemagne Empire in 814 AD

10.   From the 9th century, France was ruled by a succession of kings for more than 900 years. The most famous of these kings was Louis XIV and during his reign France became the most powerful country in Europe.

11.   Louis XIV, known as the "Sun King", reigned for 72 years (1643 - 1715) - longer than any other European monarch. He brought a golden age of art and literature to France and is perhaps best known for building the magnificent palace at Versailles, which was a great center of culture and a symbol of the king's immense power.

Louis XIV

12. In the 18th century, most of the French population were extremely poor and when the king, Louis XVI, decided to raise taxes the people became very angry and rose up against their rulers. The French Revolution was about to begin.

13. The revolution in France started on July 14 1789, when hundreds of men attacked the Bastille prison in Paris. The soldiers guarding the prison where defeated and prisoners were set free.

The "Storming of the Bastille"

14. Following the "Storming of the Bastille", the revolution spread to other parts of France as the people killed many of the ruling classes and took over their properties. The monarchy and nobility were eventually swept away and the French people were able to form their own parliament.

15. The violence and unrest of the revolution lasted for 10 years, during which time many thousands of people were killed, including King Louis and his wife, Marie Antoinette.

16. The revolution finally ended in 1799, when an army general, Napoleon Bonaparte, took control and declared himself leader of France.

Napoleon Bonaparte

17. In 1804, Napoleon made himself the Emperor of France and set about invading other European countries to create a French empire.

18. Over the next 10 years, Napoleon conquered much of Europe and was at war with Britain, Austria and Russia. He was finally defeated at the Battle of Waterloo in 1815 and imprisoned on the remote island of St. Helena, 4,500 miles (7,250 km) away in the middle of the South Atlantic Ocean.

19. The French Revolution completely changed the way France was governed. The country became a republic, which meant that the French people could choose a president and other politicians to run the country, rather than being ruled over by an unelected king or queen.

20. Like other European countries, France had built an overseas empire over the centuries, but a series of wars with Britain in the 18th century had seen the French lose most of their colonies.

21. The 19th century saw France rebuild her empire, taking over countries in Africa, Southeast Asia and the South Pacific Ocean.

22. By 1900, the French Empire was the second largest in the world after the British Empire, with control of more than 100 million people.

23. In 1870, France went to war with against an alliance of German states, which resulted in a crushing victory for the Germans and the unification of those states into one nation. There was now a deep distrust between France and Germany, producing a very unstable peace which came to an end just over 40 years later.

Victory celebrations in Germany in 1871

24. In the early 20th century, there was tension not just between Germany and France, but between countries throughout Europe. In 1914 the tension snapped with the outbreak of World War One.

25. Soon after the war started, the German army marched through Belgium towards the French capital, Paris, but they were halted 30 miles from the city by the French army and its British allies. Both sides stood their ground and the fighting continued for four years, not just in Europe, but across the world with the loss of millions of lives.

26. The war ended in 1918 with a humiliating defeat for Germany. France and her allies punished the Germans heavily for its part in the war, causing resentment which was to lead to an even worse war 20 years later.

27. In 1939, the German leader, Adolf Hitler, decided to take revenge for his country's defeat in 1918. His army invaded Belgium again but this time it took just six weeks to reach Paris and conquer France.

German soldiers in Paris in 1940

28. The world was at war again and it wasn't until six years later that armies from the United States, Britain and Canada landed on the beaches of northern France before marching to Paris and freeing the country from German control.

29. When World War Two was over, the countries of Europe knew they must never go to war with each other again. The Council of Europe was formed which eventually became the European Union. Today, France is an important member of the Union and the major countries of Europe have been at peace since 1945.

The European Union flag

Climate & Landscape

30. The landscape of France is varied. There are the high cliffs and sandy beaches of the northern coast, the spectacular mountain ranges in the south and east, and vast areas of low-lying fertile farmland.

31. More than a quarter of France is covered in forests, especially in the south-east. There are more trees in France than anywhere else in Europe except for Scandinavia.

32. The mountain ranges of France include the French Alps, which separate France from Italy, and the Pyrenees, which form a natural border with Spain.

The Pyrenees

33.   The Alps are home to the highest mountain in Europe. The summit of Mont Blanc, which means "White Mountain", is 15,770 feet (4,807 m) above sea level.

34.   Much of central France is covered by an ancient mountain range called the Massif Central. It covers nearly one sixth of the country and is peppered with extinct volcanoes which last erupted 10,000 years ago.

35.   There are four main rivers in France - the Loire, the Seine, the Garonne and the Rhône. The longest of these is the Loire, which flows for 629 miles (1,012 km) from its source in the Massif Central until it reaches the Atlantic Ocean. The river flows through some of the most fertile and beautiful parts of the country.

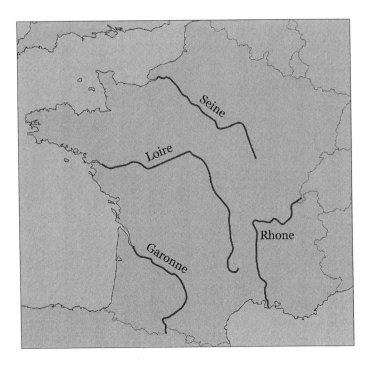

The major rivers of France

36. Most of France has a climate of warm summers and mild winters, although the Mediterranean climate of the south brings hot summers and warm winters. The mountain regions are very cold during the winter and are covered in snow at this time of year.

37. During the winter and spring, a strong wind known as the "Mistral" blows from north to south down the Rhône valley in southern France. It can last for days and reach speeds of up to 62 mph (100 kph), which causes trees to grow leaning to the south.

Culture & Sport

38. The French are known for their elegance and style, and the capital city of Paris is one of the world's great centers of fashion. Clothes buyers from all over the world visit the Paris Fashion Week every year to see the latest styles.

39. World famous French fashion designers include Christian Dior, Yves Saint Laurent, Coco Chanel and Louis Vitton.

40. Some of the world's best known museums and art galleries can be found in France. The Louvre in Paris is perhaps the most famous, attracting more than nine million visitors every year to see its priceless exhibits.

The Louvre

41. For hundreds of years, France has produced great music composers. Some of the most well known are Maurice Ravel, Claude Debussy and Georges Bizet. Foreign composers such as Chopin and Stravinsky were attracted to Paris to live and work there.

42. One of the most famous sculptors ever is Auguste Rodin, who was born in Paris in 1840. His most well known work, "The Thinker", can be seen at the Musée Rodin in his home city.

Rodin's "The Thinker"

43. Every year in the southern coastal resort of Cannes, the world's most famous film festival takes place. Film makers come from all over the world hoping to win the prestigious "Palme d'Or" ("The Golden Hand").

44. A style of painting known as 'Impressionism' was started in France in the 19th century. Led by Claude Monet and Auguste Renoir, the Impressionists rejected the traditional way of painting to try to capture the effects of light in nature.

"Poppies" by Monet

45. Soccer is the most popular sport in France. Frenchman Jules Rimet was responsible for the first World cup competition in 1930 and the winner's trophy was named after him in his honor.

46. The French national soccer team is known as 'Les Bleus' (The Blues) after the color of the shirts they play in. Les Bleus became world soccer champions for the second time in 1998 when the World Cup was held in France.

47. The French invented motor racing in 1894, when cars raced each other between the cities of Paris and Rouen. These first races were called 'Grand Prix', a term which is still used in Formula One today.

48. France is home to the most famous cycle race in the world, the Tour de France. It takes place every July when around 150 riders race each other over 2,235 miles (3,600 km) along the roads of France before reaching the finishing line in Paris.

Riders in the 2012 Tour de France

Paris

49. The capital of France, Paris, is one of the world's major cities. It is home to more than 2 million people and is an important center for fashion, culture, art, food and shopping.

50. Paris is one of the most popular tourist destinations in the world, with more than 40 million people visiting every year.

51. Paris has been France's capital for more than 1,500 years and the center of the city has many historic and spectacular buildings.

52. On an island in the middle of the River Seine, which runs through the center of Paris, is the magnificent medieval Notre-Dame Cathedral. The building took more than 100 years to build and is one of the biggest and best-known churches in the world.

Notre-Dame Cathedral

53. A short distance from Notre-Dame on the north bank of the Seine is the Louvre, which is one of the largest and oldest museums in the world. Among its 35,000 priceless treasures is the world's most famous painting, Leonardo da Vinci's "Mona Lisa".

Leonardo da Vinci's "Mona Lisa"

54. The tallest building in Paris is the Eiffel Tower. The 985 feet (300 m) high iron tower was built in 1889 to celebrate the 100th anniversary of the French Revolution. It was only meant to be there for 20 years but is still standing more than 100 years later!

The Eiffel Tower

55. At the end of the Avenue des Champs-Élysée stands the 162 feet (49.5m) high Arc de Triomphe. It was built in 1836 to commemorate soldiers who had fought for France, and at 6.30 every evening a ceremony is held to honor those who have died fighting for their country.

The Arc de Triomphe

56. In 1682, the French King, Louis XIV, moved his entire court from Paris to his newly built palace at Versailles. 17th century Versailles was a small village but today it is a wealthy suburb of Paris and home to one of the most spectacular palaces ever built.

The palace at Versailles

Food & Drink

57. The French love food and wine and every region of the country has its own style of cooking which uses local produce. Provence in the south uses lots of garlic, olive oil and herbs, while Normandy in the north is famous for its seafood, apples and cream.

58. There are more than 300 different types of French cheeses and French people eat more cheese than any other country in the world. Brie and Camembert are well-known soft cheeses while a famous hard cheese is Roquefort.

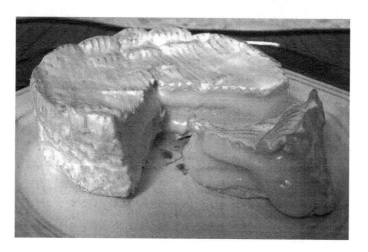

Camembert cheese

59. The French eat bread with most meals and each region produces its own type of bread. The most famous of French breads is the "baguette", which means "little stick", which can be up to three feet (one meter) long!

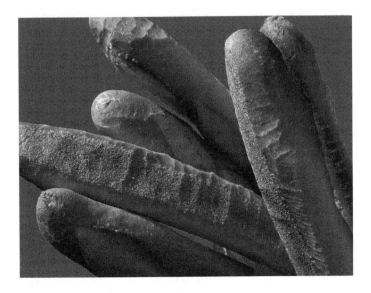

Baguettes

60. French dishes which are famous throughout the world include Boeuf Bourguignon (a beef stew from Burgundy), Ratatouille (a vegetable stew from the South of France) and Coq au Vin (chicken braised in wine).

Ratatouille

61. One of the favorite foods of the French is the truffle, which is a fungus that grows underground. Pigs and dogs are specially trained to find the buried truffles by using their strong sense of smell.

62. Some of the more unusual foods that the French eat are "les escargot" (snails), "la viande de cheval" (horsemeat), "les cuisses de grenouille" (frogs' legs) and "steak tartare" (minced raw horsemeat or beef).

63. The climate of France is ideal for growing vines, which wine is made from. Different regions produce different types of wine, from sparkling champagne in the north to the rich red wines of the south.

64.   The French love to drink wine with their meals and it is said that the average French person drinks more than 60 liters of wine every year, more than in any other country in the world.

Assorted France Facts

65. The French flag, known as the "tricolore", meaning "three colors" was first used during the revolution of 1789. The blue of the flag represents Saint Martin, the white is the color of French heroine, Joan of Arc, and the red represents Saint Denis, the patron saint of Paris.

The French flag

66. Every year, on July 14, France commemorates one of the most important events in its history with a national holiday. It was on that date in 1789 that the storming of the Bastille took place to begin the French Revolution. "Bastille Day" sees every town and city in the country celebrate with parties and fireworks.

67. The guillotine was used to cut the heads off thousands of people during the French Revolution. Invented by Dr. Joseph-Ignace Guillotin, it was thought to be a humane way of execution. The guillotine was last used in 1977 before the death penalty was abolished in France four years later.

68. Major French inventions include the parachute, the hot air balloon, Braille, the stethoscope, the aqualung and canned food.

Hot air balloons

69. In June 1944, the Normandy coast of northern France saw one of the largest military operations ever undertaken when 135,000 soldiers from the United States, Great Britain and Canada stormed ashore from 6,000 ships. The D-Day Landings eventually led to the freeing of France from German occupation and the end of World War Two.

70. The Statue of Liberty, which stands on Liberty Island in New York, was a gift from France to the American people in 1886 to celebrate the end of the American Civil War and the abolition of slavery in the United States.

The Statue of Liberty

71. In 1971 a group of French physicians formed "Médecin sans Frontières" to provide medical care in international emergencies. The organization was awarded the Nobel Peace Prize in 1999.

72. Frenchman Baron Pierre de Coubertin was responsible for the staging of the first modern Olympic Games in Athens in 1896. Paris hosted the Olympics four years later and again in 1924. France hosted the first Winter Olympics in 1924 and again in 1968 and 1988.

For more in the Fascinating Facts For Kids series, please visit:

www.fascinatingfactsforkids.com

Illustration Attributions

Map of France
Superbenjamin

A cave painting at Lascaux
{{PD-1923}}

The Charlemange Empire in 814 AD
wolpertinger, Tsui

Louis XIV
{{PD-1923}}

The "Storming of the Bastille"
{{PD-1923}}

Napoleon Bonaparte
{{PD-1923}}

Victory celebrations in Germany in 1871
{{PD-1923}}

German soldiers in Paris in 1940
Bundesarchiv, Bild 183-L05487 / CC-BY-SA 3.0

The Pyrenees
90664717@N00 at http://www.flickr.com

Riders in the 2012 Tour de France
Josh Hallett from Winter Haven, FL, USA

Notre-Dame Cathedral
Zuffe

The Arc de Triomphe
Benh LIEU SONG

Camembert cheese
NJGJ

Ratatouille
Marcus Guimarães

Hot air balloons
Tomas Castelazo

17627624R00022

Made in the USA
Middletown, DE
27 November 2018